To Nelly

Soaring Above the Storms
Volume 1
Poems to Inspire Joy and Peace
By
Effie Darlene Barba

Dedicated to

First and foremost, I dedicate my life to Jesus Christ, who died to set me free. He rose again the third day so that I might be justified, finding in Him my only hope of fully Being. He is my life, my joy, my everything. Without Him, I am nothing but a sinner in search of existence. Nothingness would be my name apart from Him.

Beyond that I thank God for Pedro Barba, Jr who God used to teach me about sacrificial, unconditional love. It was through my life with him I began to understand the depth, length, and breadth of God's love for me.

I also dedicate this book to my dear mother who first introduced me to Christ and who has shown me what unconditional love really looks like.

And to my children: Melissa, Alberto, and Ronald who have truly been God's greatest blessings to me.

I thank God each day for all He has so richly given me in life, even the trials. For amid the trials I came to know Him better and to know what it is to have Abiding Steadfast Joy that carries me through life's storms. He makes me soar above the storms by His mighty power, His strength, and His abiding presence with me.

Unless otherwise noted, scripture is from the King James Version Bible

Table of Contents

Family & Friends

Introduction

I have always been drawn to music, particularly those songs that express the depth of my emotions at any given time. Whenever I was caught up in a whirlwind of sorrow, pain, or emotional conflict, as I went to bed, I prayed. Then somewhere around 2 am I would awaken with the words of a song playing in my head. Most often it was a song I had not thought of for a long time. Yet, it was the perfect song to answer whatever trial I faced. I always considered these as gifts from God. Once awakened, then a scripture verse would pop into my head. Peace would overtake my worried mind and I would fall back to sleep.

So it was, music allowed me to feel the depths of my sorrow while simultaneously cradling me safely in God's arms.

The Lord, your God in your midst, the Mighty One, will save; He will rejoice over you with gladness, He will quiet you with His love, He will rejoice over you with singing. (Zephaniah 3:17 NKJV)

The first time I wrote a poetic song was when my brother died. My grief was overwhelming! He was taken suddenly in a car accident. My husband refused to let my children go with me which caused me great worry leaving them alone with him; but that is another story. Everything was made worse because out of nowhere, with no precipitation, my husband declared he was filing for divorce as soon as I returned. This as he drove me to the airport. I felt lost, frightened, and alone. Grief, fear, and pain gripped my heart. Then quietly softly as the plane carried me to my destination, I began to hear this song in my head. I had nothing to write it down on; but it kept playing over and over for days until finally I sat down and wrote it onto a piece of paper and tucked it away for another day.

When I First Came to Know Him

When I first came to know him
So many years ago
I vowed that I would serve him
With heart and mind and soul
Then I found that in my strength
I would but only fail
Then He came and He told me
As we walked down life's trail

1st chorus
I'll be your strength when you are weary
Your hope when skies are gray
I'll be your faith when yours is failing
And your light on each dark day
I'll be the love to your lonely heart
When it's breaking in despair
I'll be all in all your everything
If you look to me in prayer

I strove on in my strength
And strayed so very far
Until my life was broken
And sin had left its scar
Then I cried, Oh, my Father
How deeply I have failed
Then He came and He held me
And His love prevailed

2nd Chorus
Now He's my strength when I am weary
My hope when skies are gray
He is my faith when mine is failing
And my light on each dark day
He is the love to my lonely heart
When it's breaking in despair
He is all in all my everything
When I look to him in prayer

Now if you have strayed from
Or never knew His love
Then turn your eyes toward Jesus
And seek Him from above
He will take all your brokenness
And fill it with Himself
He will take all your sin away
And fill each empty shelf.

3rd Chorus
He'll be your strength when you are weary
Your hope when skies are gray
He'll be your faith when yours is failing
And your light on each dark day
He'll be the love to your lonely heart
When it's breaking in despair
He'll be all in all your everything
If you look to Him in prayer

After that moment, years passed before I began to hear poetic verses in my head again, though I walked through many trials. Oh, by the way, Pete did not divorce me. In fact, he never mentioned it again, so neither did I. And my children? They were fine when I returned from my brother's funeral. We lived many more years together through the ups and downs of life. Then tragically, Pete died. I walked for a long time with a grief that seemed unbearable. Yet, for the sake of the children, I had to keep walking, smiling, and living. Then through the years that followed I faced many other trials including cancer, ulcerative colitis, and a multitude of surgeries. With so much illness there came the financial trials. Yet God's grace gave me the strength to keep working. He always provided a way, even when I thought none could be found. Indeed, the illness drove me closer to Him as I began to get up early in the mornings to be alone in His presence. It was pain that woke me. Yet it was the time with Him that gave me the strength to go on. His presence overrode the pain. Then, with His strength to lift me up, I would go to work. Money was tight; but there was always just enough.

Throughout all the storms of life, God would comfort me in the night with hymns and Bible verses.

I so loved music! It was as if the songs knew the me, my story and provided an answer to my pain. Furthermore, the songs gave me a reason to rejoice. Still, I did not myself think in poetic form again until… Suddenly, in a moment of devastating heartbreak, once more I found words forming in my mind that brought me great comfort as I began to write them down. This was that poem.

To God-My Love, My Hope, My Joy

My life-so filled with hopes and dreams

Lay shattered at Your feet

So many tears, so many pains

I laid before Your seat

Can I look upon Your face of love?

And question what You've done?

For You have been my only hope

My only morning sun!

You've seen my heart when crushed with pain

Your hands have held it tight

When I have been so weak, so frail

You've shown Your strength, Your might

You've held me close within Your arms

When darkness filled my night

And when I could not see my way

Your eyes, they gave me sight

I lay my life within Your hands

That You may heal my soul

And keep my eyes upon You Lord

That I may reach Your goal

Shine forth Your grace, Your mercy Lord

And let me be Your light

That all may see Your eyes of love

The blind, they might have sight

Let not the sorrows, nor the pains

Bring bitterness within

And give me strength to walk this path

Protect my heart from sin

I lay my heart, my soul, my dreams

Before Your throne of love

I lift my eyes to You, My God

And seek Your will above

You are the only one I need

To fill my heart with glee

It is Your face, my one true love

Tis all I need to see

So, lift me up and hold me close

Reveal Your love divine

That through the holes within my heart

A world might see You shine

And if the sorrows of my past

Can touch a wayward one

I thank you Lord for each dark path

That lead them to Your son

I praise You now from mountains high

For each dark path I've trod

Twas there I found Your heart, Your love

Twas there I found You God

What great and wondrous joy I know

Because You are my king

And though the path I cannot see

My heart will trust and sing

A song of praise unto You Lord

Who knows what's best for me!

You'll hold my hand and lead me on

In darkness, I can see

Your love, Your help, Your guiding hand

Is all I'll ever need

So, hold me close unto Your path

For this is all I plead

I'll skip with joy along this path

Though darkness may surround

Because I know You hold my hand

My feet will ne'er touch ground

I cannot fall outside Your love

I cannot lose my way

I'll hold my broken dreams once more

And see them real, one day

A song of praise unto You Lord

Who knows what's best for me!

You'll hold my hand and lead me on

In darkness, I can see

Your love, Your help, Your guiding hand

Is all I'll ever need

So, hold me close unto Your path

For this is all I plead

After that, I found often that when I was most distressed or most impassioned, words would form within my mind to comfort me. And so, poetry became an outlet, a means of expressing all that I could not otherwise say. Things that I feared to voice became a part of a poetic verse instead. There, I felt God's presence, it was as though He cradled me in His arms of love and sang His comforting words over me. I pray that these words also bring comfort to you.

As time went by there came moments in which the poems came with humor, passion, and love as well. For me it became a way to express or say what I could not otherwise find the right words to say. There are times when I wish for a poem and it will not come. So, I have learned I cannot force a poem to be written. There may be long periods in which no poems come to me. Then, out of the blue, a poem will begin to take form, and I must write it down to finish later or lose it completely.

Bible Study, Prayer, and time alone with God inspire me to write. It has been through many trials, that I have come to cherish God as my greatest treasure. He is my source of joy, peace, hope, and love.

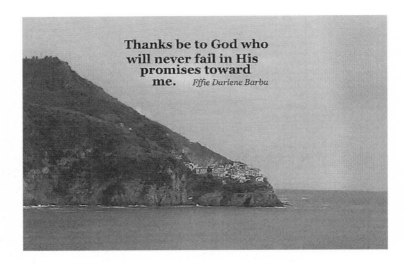

Thanks be to God who
will never fail in His
promises toward
me. *Effie Darlene Barba*

Songs of Praise

Call to Me, and I will answer you, and
show you great and mighty things
which you do not know.

Jeremiah 33:3 NKJV

A Talk with God

Oh, let me Lord Delight in You
And lay all else I hold aside
For no desire could mean as much
As hear Your voice, to feel your touch
And in Your arms abide

I feel the safety of your arms
Surrounding me throughout each storm
And when the bitter winter wind
Would bid my very spirit bend
Your breath will keep me warm

Forgive me Lord, this fragile heart
Sometimes desires too much
Forgetting You are all I need
Then comes my tears, my plead
To stop and feel Your touch

3

I then can hear your gentle laugh

The love within Your voice

"My child I love you evermore

My gifts on you I freely pour

The best for you my choice"

Oh, Lord I want to stay right here

And sit here at Your feet

To never step away from You

And then I cannot lose my view

No chance for fear, defeat

"But child I ask then who would go

To tell the wounded broken heart

That I their lonely heart would mend

If not but you, who can I send?

If you refuse to start"

Then Father, Dear, I must say yes
To go and run Your bidding do
And You will cast aside my fears
Your hand will wipe away my tears
And keep my eyes on You

I know that You go with me now
You're ever present in my heart
I feel Your joy arise within
I feel Your wondrous strength again
Your love will ne'er depart

Blessed be the God and Father
of our Lord Jesus Christ who has
blessed us with all spiritual
blessing in heavenly places in
Christ

Ephesians 1:3

All These Years

I thank you Lord for all these years
For every laugh and even tears
Your Wondrous Grace has led the way
And pulled me close when I did stray
My life has truly been so blessed
Your joy, Your hope, Your love possessed
This heart of mine-You've held me tight
Through sun kissed days and dark of night
What wondrous gifts you've given me
The love and joy of family
What mercy, grace on me did shine
You chose these children to be mine
What wondrous smile upon Your !
To gift me with such love and grace!!
Beyond all this You then did send
Each precious one that I call friend
Like angels on this earth to guide
Friends in which I could confide
One truth in which I must attest

You have given me Your very best

I thank you Lord for all You have done

But most of all for your dear Son

He gave His all to ransom me

That blessed I am eternally

"Father, forgive them, for they know not what they do."

R. BARRA

I hear this most gentle whisper
from the One I never guessed
would speak to me: "I took the
world off your shoulders

Psalm 81:5 (MSG)

Whispers of Love

Whispers of Love flowing all through my life
Even in moments of sorrow or strife
Whispers that came in the dark of the night
Promising Joy with the new morning light
Whispers of hope for the bleakest of day
"Love will find strength and will find its way"
Into your heart and grow from within
Until it flows forth rejoicing and then
Suddenly out of those long and sad years
Love does spring forth out of fountains of tears
Into rivers of joy bursting forth then to see
That love had been there abiding in me

Oh, thank you dear Lord for teaching me love
As Your spirit descends with the wings of a dove
And gathered the pieces of this shattered heart
To weave it with steel, Your Glory impart
A Picture so rare, its beauty unmasked
A portrait of you made in brilliant stained glass

Your love had been there inside of me
Even when I had been too blind to see
Whispers of love, it was You all along
Holding me close, I am Your love song!

The angel went forth and told Elijah, "Go forth and stand upon the mount before the Lord. And behold, the Lord passed by, and a great and strong wind rent the mountains, and brake in pieces the rocks before the Lord; but the Lord was not in the wind: and after the wind an earthquake; but the Lord was not in the earthquake. And after the earthquake a fire; but the Lord was not in the fire: And after the fire a still small voice. And it was so, when Elijah heard it, that he wrapped his face in his mantle and went out and stood in the entering in of the cave. And behold, there came a voice unto him, and said, What doest thou here, Elijah? I Kings 19: 11-13

My heart is steadfast, O God, my heart is steadfast; I will sing and give praise.

Awake, my glory!

Awake, lute and harp!

I will awaken the dawn.

I will praise You, O Lord, among the peoples; I will sing to You among the nations.

Psalm 57:7-9

Awaken to Joy

Awaken, Awaken Oh heart of mine

Today has arrived so rich and Divine

Such Joy overflows into a new song

"By Grace I am Saved and By Grace I belong"

Wherever I go—whatever I do

Let Your Glorious Hope be all that I view

Such awe and wonder you place in my path

While never your anger-- never your wrath

Oh, Marvelous Grace that fills me with glee

Before your dear throne I have this one plea

That your love flows forth to all whom I meet

Seeing Your Glory, they fall at Your feet

Lord let me be a reflection of You

In all that I say and all that I do

Let the Grace that You freely gave to me

Be the Grace that I give to those I see

Let Love guide my feet wherever I go

Your joy and Your hope be all that does show

And one day, Dear Lord, when this earth I leave

Don't let those who knew me one moment grieve

Because they know that you are my treasure

And being with you my greatest pleasure

Let the life that I lived be an echo so true

Of the Grace and the love that I found in You

Awaken, Awaken Oh heart of mine

Today has arrived so rich and divine

Such Joy overflows into a new song

"By Grace I am Saved and By Grace I belong"

When I consider Your heavens, the work of Your fingers, the moon and the stars, which You have ordained. What is man that You are mindful of him, and the son of man that You visit him? For You have made him a little lower than the angels, and You have crowned him with glory and honor.

O Lord, our Lord, how excellent is Your name in all the earth!

Psalm 8: 3-5,9

Because I See thy Gift of Grace

A pilgrim's journey through this land

Through meadow's soft and desert sand

Beside the gentle bubbling streams

With flowers kissed by sunlit beams

Or rushing, roaring waterfalls

Whose beauty gasps and danger calls

Twinkling stars, the dark of night

They guide my way and shed Your light

The gentle breeze across my face

Whispering words of God's sweet Grace

Creator Lord with all You do

Whom else on earth could I pursue

For all I have and all I am

Is due to You—My precious lamb

You chose to die and pay my price

In You I find my paradise

And now I see through different eyes

This course on earth no more disguise

Its beauties shine, your glory clear

I feel your breath, your warmth so near

To warm the chill within my soul

Like fireplace lit in winter's snow

You blessed my life with love's sweet kiss

That hope and joy arise amidst

The darkest trials I may face

Because I see thy Gift of Grace

The steadfast love the the Lord never ceases; His mercies never come to an end; they are new every morning. Great is Your Faithfulnerss!

The Lord is my portion," says my soul, "therefore, I will hope in Him.

Lamentations 3:22-24 (ESV)

Bright New Day

Let the bells ring forth a joyous sound

Of Love and hope to all around

The past is gone, to be no more

Today, new dreams to seek, explore

Just like the dawning of new light

Brings with it beams of strength and might

That stretch like arms to fill the sky

With rays of hope for you and I

Each day with mercies new God gives

Beginnings bright, His spirit lives

Within our hearts to comfort, cheer

To know that God has drawn us near

Because in Christ we have new life

No longer trapped in sin and strife

He cloaked me in His righteousness

That I might now be filled with bliss

The God of Israel said,

The Rock of Israel spoke to me:

"He who rules over men must be just,

Ruling in the fear of God

And he shall be like the light of the morning

When the sun rises,

A morning without clouds,

Like the tender grass springing out of the earth,

Like the tender grass springing out of the earth

By clear shining after rain."

Although my house is not so with God,

Yet He has made with me an everlasting

Covenant,

Ordered in all things and secure.

For this is my salvation and all my desire.

Will He not make it increase?

2 Samuel 23:3-5 NKJV

Thou hast turned for me my mourning into dancing: thou hast put off my sackcloth, and girded me with gladness; to the end that my glory may sing praise to thee, and not be silent. O Lord my God I will give thanks unto thee forever.

Psalm 30:11-12

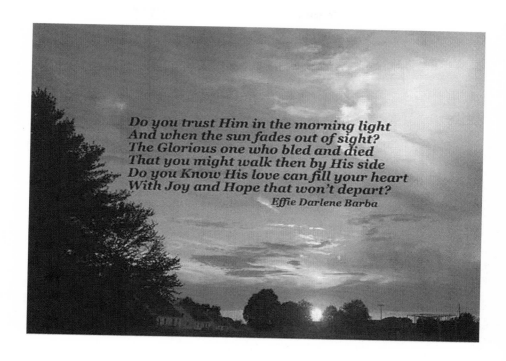

Do you trust Him in the morning light
And when the sun fades out of sight?
The Glorious one who bled and died
That you might walk then by His side
Do you Know His love can fill your heart
With Joy and Hope that won't depart?

Effie Darlene Barba

I will greatly rejoice in the Lord, my soul shall be joyful in my God; for He hath clothed me with the garments of salvation, He hath covered me with the robe of righteousness, as a bridegroom decketh himself with ornaments, and as a bride adorneth herself with her jewels.

Isaiah 61:10

The Name of Joy

With Glorious shout, I must proclaim
True Joy does have a name
A name so sweet so filled with love
Indwelt with power from above
That all before His name must bow
Yet, Majesty saw me somehow
Thus Jesus Christ, He died for me
That I this wretch might be set free
From quilt laid chains that bound despair
This heart so caught in sin's dark lair
Set Free by Grace-now lifts in flight
My path illumined by His light
To rise above my shame to soar
Drawn by His Glory evermore
And cloaked with righteousness not mine
The Mystery of Grace Divine
That all my heart did once desire
I cast into the murky mire
That I might go wherever He might lead
And to His will long to concede
My voice resounding joyous strains
Amidst these earthly trials, pains
My eyes are fixed upon my Lord
My heart in His with one accord
Held firmly by His Mighty Hand
That I, in victory may stand
And one day on that distant shore
I will be with Him for evermore
With Glorious shout, I must proclaim
True Joy does have a name

For though we walk in the flesh, we do not war according to flesh. For the weapons of our warfare are not carnal but mighty in God for pulling down strongholds, casting down arguments and every high thing that exalts itself against the knowledge of God, bringing every thought into captivity to the obedience of Christ.

2 Corinthians 10:3-5 (NET)

The Key

God's Spirit does within me lie
The strength on which I must rely
The blood of Christ did set me free
That I might live in liberty

Yet, liberty demands my all
Surrender to the Spirit's call
That filled with joy from Christ within
I rise above myself and sin

His presence filling me with love
That I might soar on clouds above
The clamor, hate, and jealous rage
That holds me in this wretched cage

Oh, that my mind might comprehend
Only His love can ever mend
This heart so broken, filled with pride
The evil darkness that I hide

The depth and breadth of Love He gave

As on the Cross He died to save

Me from the wretchedness within

To wash me white from crimson sin

Dear Lord, please take all of me

Fill my heart, that I might see

Only You, and nothing more

So, like an eagle I might soar

Your Spirit as my only guide

In Christ, I rest-in Him abide

Therein I rise to heights unknown

While prostrate lie before thy throne

Oh, fill me God with all of You

Until You are all that I view

Your Glorious Light might then shine bright

To this dark world in need of light

Where sin abounded, grace did much more abound. That as sin hath reigned unto death, even so might grace reign through righteousness unto eternal life by Jesus Christ our Lord.

Romans 5: 20-21

Transforming Grace

Transforming Grace, how could it be
That you should choose someone like me
And with one touch these blind eyes free
A glimpse of Glory's love to see

A mind so filled with doubt and fear
Transformed to peace as you draw near
The darkened winding path now clear
As whisper of your voice I hear

I cannot fathom why you sought
Someone like me, Salvation bought
That from this rubbish thou hast wrought
A life now filled with Your dear thought

So, take this selfish heart you found
And with your gentle love surround
That kindness might pour forth abound
And songs of praise the only sound

So, mold me by your righteous hand
That firm within Your truth I stand
And trusting all that you have planned
Your joy I sing throughout this land

But what things were gain to me, those I counted
loss for Christ. Yea, doubtless, and I count all
things but loss for the excellency of the knowledge
of Christ Jesus my Lord: for whom I have suffered
the loss of all things, and do count them but dung,
that I may win Christ. And be found in Him, not
having my own righteousness, which is of the law,
but that which is through the faith of Christ, the
righteousness which is of God by faith: That I may
know Him, and the power of His resurrection, and
the fellowship of His sufferings, being made
conformable unto His death. Philippians 3:7-10

Whatever the Cost, Your Praise I Will Sing

It was a cross that set me free
And purchased there my victory
While Jesus there my case did plead
So willingly to die and bleed
He never shirked such wretched pain
He bore my sin, it's crimson stain
To cloak me with His righteousness
Though I am merely nothingness

I have no Glory I can bring
No accolades of which to sing
Until I find my place in Him
From darkness, then His light can beam
Upon a World so filled with need
That then my heart desires to plead
On bended knees, their case in prayer
I willingly my cross do bear

Whatever sorrow I must face

To point the lost to God's dear Grace

Dear Lord, my life I give to You

To do with as You wish to do

My journey guided by Your hand

Your strength alone on which I stand

So, take my life and let it be

Whatever You desire for me

And If for me you choose a cross

That I might count all gain but loss

Compared to You, my Lord and King

My Joy will still Your praises sing

Rejoice in the Lord, O ye righteous: for praise is comely for the upright. Praise the Lord with harp: sing unto Him with the psaltery and an instrument of ten strings. Sing unto Him a new song; play skillfully with a loud noise. For the word of the Lord is right: and all His works are done in truth. He Loveth righteousness and judgment. The earth is full of the goodness of the Lord. Psalm 33:1-5

A Thanksgiving Day Song

As I look back over all my years
Amazing Joy or sometimes tears
Each winding road, an Act of Grace
That I might seek Your Glorious Face
And as my life draws nearer to You
I came to know Your words were True
Those Words that drew me near your heart
And bid me stay and ne'er depart

Chorus:
Oh let my joy then ever be
A song of Grace that sets men free
From all the chains that tightly bind
Or foolish pride that makes hearts blind
Thanksgiving would be greater still
Each day conformed unto Your will
A truly thankful heart be mine
When Humbly filled with Joy Divine

II
How foolish I at times have been
My faltering steps and wretched sin
I searched this world in hopes to find
A love so true, so sweet and kind
I did not see the tears You shed
Consider that for me You bled

39

No greater treasure could be mine
As Your beloved, our hearts entwined

Chorus:
Oh let my joy then ever be
A song of Grace that sets men free
From all the chains that tightly bind
Or foolish pride that makes hearts blind
Thanksgiving would be greater still
Each day conformed unto Your will
A truly thankful heart be mine
When Humbly filled with Joy Divine

III
Lord, hold me tight within Your arms
Tis there I'm safe from all life's harms
My head pressed firm upon Your chest
For just a moment let me rest
And let me gaze at Your Sweet smile
As on we walk each winding mile
My dearest love, You are my King
It is for You I must now sing

Chorus:
Oh let my joy then ever be
A song of Grace that sets men free

From all the chains that tightly bind
Or foolish pride that makes hearts blind
Thanksgiving would be greater still
Each day conformed unto Your will
A truly thankful heart be mine
When Humbly filled with Joy Divine

And Elisha prayed, and said, Lord, I pray thee, open his eyes, that he may see. And the Lord opened the eyes of the young man; and he saw: and, behold, the mountain was full of horses and chariots of fire round about Elisha.

2 Kings 6:17

LORD, Open My Eyes Each Day to See

We hurry here and scurry there
No thought of God, our friend
We think this world important now
Our life will never end
Our words and thoughts important, right
While anger grows within
"For I deserve a better life"
Our pride bequests our sin

Chorus:
LORD, open my eyes each day to see
Your Glory bright surrounding me
That I might cast aside my pride
And in Your Righteousness, Abide

Oh LORD, the more I know of you

The more my heart desires to see

And as Your glory grows within

Then, less I think of me

Your Word, it draws me closer in

Transforming my life's view

Until Your precious, wondrous face

Is All that I pursue

Chorus:

LORD, open my eyes each day to see

Your Glory bright surrounding me

That I might cast aside my pride

And in Your Righteousness, Abide

Amazing Grace that draws me near

Sometimes through trials dark

Whate'er it takes, my God please bring

Your flames of love to spark

Let fires of passion for your word

Take o'er this heart of mine

Until to darkest night of men

Your Love and Glory Shine

Chorus:

LORD, open my eyes each day to see

Your Glory bright surrounding me

That I might cast aside my pride

And in Your Righteousness, Abide

† † †

Hope and Faith for Life's Raging Storms

The Lord draws nigh to the broken hearted and
saveth such as be of a contrite spirit

Psalm 34:18

The Song of a Butterfly

A little girl had called Your name

Began to feast upon Your word

And like a caterpillar came

To cherish comfort, truth was blurred

I thought that if I did what's right

You'd give me all my heart's delight

Had I forgotten it was Grace

That had saved a worm such as I

Within my heart pride took its place

Then I believed as truth the lie

That if You loved me as Your dear

49

You'd only fill my life with cheer

Above all else my one desire

To find the one who'd love me true

Enduring all I flamed that fire

And there He was, a gift from You

A human heart with broken soul

The pain of which did take its toll

Yet, willing heart my love stood firm

I bade you Lord to give me strength

Your love for me you did affirm

Unveiling all its depth and length

And then You took my earthly love

To be with you- Your home above

My sorrow came like bitter rain

I searched for love again to find

Attempts to love I did but feign

Until to loneliness resigned

I cannot tell you now the why

Despite Your love I still did cry

With Broken Heart-I drew within

And built a hard cocoon like shell

How was it that I thought therein?

I'd safe from pain and sorrow dwell

There within the dark cold wall

I heard God's voice, I heard You call

In darkness there I felt Your Grace

I struggled, Lord your will to see

And there I saw Your love filled face

This gave me strength to then break free

So there I'd sealed myself to die

And now emerged a butterfly

Oh wondrous Joy I know is mine

And Love abounding in this heart

Your Mercy, Grace and Glory Shine

Upon my life You did impart

The broken moments You did will

That I might fly above the hill

And now, Dear God; Your love in me

No longer wrought with fear or need

This heart of mine has been set free

To pour forth love in word and deed

To those I meet along this way

And fly with joy in You today.

Out of the depths have I cried unto thee, O Lord.
Lord, hear my voice: let thine ears be attentive to
the voice of my supplications. If thou, Lord
shouldest mark iniquities, O Lord, who shall stand?
But there is forgiveness with thee, that thou
mayest be feared. I wait for the Lord, my soul
doth wait, and in His word do I hope.

Psalm 130:1-5

In Christ, I am God's own Beloved

Accused, Condemned in eyes of men

Rejected, hated for my sin

No one stopped to see my heart

Cast aside some broken part

That no one cared to see inside

The scars and sorrows that abide

A heart so filled with hopes and dreams

Of meadows green and crystal streams

Lay shattered, broken cast away

With nothing good or kind to say

Chorus

Then God's Dear Grace that loved me so

Looked deep within and bid to know

Each crevice of my heart and soul

Each broken piece to then make whole

In Christ I am set free from sin

My guilt and shame all taken in

And bore upon that rugged cross

My strength to stand though all else loss

My sins all covered by His blood

In Christ, I am God's own Beloved

How quickly men's own selfish pride

Does cast away and cast aside

A fallen one—a broken heart

Who needs your hand to help them start?

Christ had come to heal the lame

To lift their guilt and take their shame

He called the sinners to His side

To know His love, in Him abide

So why do we not give our hand

To help a fallen one to stand

So, prideful man with heart so small

Be careful lest you too shall fall

Chorus

For it was God's dear Grace that loved me so

Looked deep within and bid to know

Each crevice of my heart and soul

Each broken piece to then make whole

In Christ I am set free from sin

My guilt and shame all taken in

And bore upon that rugged cross

My strength to stand though all else loss

My sins all covered by His blood

In Christ, I am God's own Beloved

For we are His workmanship (His Masterpiece), created in Christ Jesus for good works, which God prepared beforehand that we should walk in them.

Ephesians 2:10

For whom He did foreknow, He also did predestinate to be conformed to the image of His Son

Romans 8:29

The Master Weaver

Broken threads my life you found
And with your love each piece you bound
A song of love your lips resound
With gentle hands, each thread you place
Oh, could it be, amazing grace
A picture clear, my Savior's face
What joy divine, could it be true
Each broken thread, you only knew
When woven tight would look like you

The Scarlet threads my broken heart
The deepest sorrow blues impart
Each silver thread of tears that fell
You guide my life with such detail
A brilliant gold, your love divine
My sins were washed, a white sublime
You gently weave with skillful hand
The portrait mine that you have planned

Oh, let me Lord remember this
That I might know with joy and bliss
You did ordain my every tear
That I might learn to never fear
That I might trust the weaver's hand
And on this hope and promise stand
Your love will always know what's best

Your cradling arms are where I rest

Broken threads my life you found
And with your love each piece you bound
A song of love your lips resound
With gentle hands, each thread you place
Oh could it be, amazing grace
A picture clear, my Savior's face
What joy divine, could it be true
Each broken thread, you only knew
When woven tight would look like you

In Christ we can be washed of all our sins and miraculously be born into a new and vibrant life --spiritually Alive to God.   In Christ we have the dawning of new life, hope, love and JOY.

Effie Darlene Barba

Thou wilt shew me the path of life: in thy presence
is fulness of joy; at thy right hand there are
pleasures for evermore (Eternal Joy in Him)

Psalm 16:11

All of You Eternally

Without the sorrows would I see
Your beauty rare—Your love for me?
Or would this heart be satisfied
With lesser things that build my pride.

Your love for me so great and grand
Allowed each tear as You had planned
That I might seek Your lovely face
Eager to feel your arms of grace

And now, this Joy that fills my chest
Is mine because in You I rest
Your Glory lights my every trail
My precious treasure without fail

I thought my heart would break in two
Until Your Love came into view
What mystery Your Grace Divine
My Darkest hour Your light did shine

This Joy, this hope, this love that's mine

I feel Your spirit intertwine

Within my heart to nourish me

With all of You eternally

That I may know Him and the power of His
resurrection, and the fellowship of His sufferings,
being made conformable unto His death

Philippians 3:10

Lullaby of Love

Awakened with fear I do not know why
Struggling to pray, I really must try
Thoughts whirling, twirling around in my brain
Unharnessed they fly, I cannot constrain
Screaming within all the guilt and the shame
I know it's my fault and I am to blame
Though I wanted to follow, I turned away
I was the one who had wandered astray
I struggled to find a verse from your word
To comfort my soul, a hope to be heard
There amid all my darkness, sorrow and pain
A soft, gentle sound, a song's sweet refrain
My shepherd's dear voice was calling my name
My eyes filled with tears, as nearer He came
Trapped in the thicket and thorns of my heart
I longed for release, a chance, a new start

Chorus

Then the words of His song grew ever so clear

"Hush little one, there is nothing to fear

My love for you grows with each beat of my heart

A love that cannot die nor ever depart

You are precious to me; I love you so

I laid down my life just so you would know

The depth of my love, my mercy my grace

Oh, look at me now. Look into my face

And rest, my dear love, rest here in my arms

Forever my strength will keep you from harms

Wherever you go wherever you are

My Glory will shine as your guiding star

When the sorrows of life cause you to roam

My lullaby song will lead you back home"

Forgetting His pain, the thorns He did tare

Until I was freed from that dark hidden lair

He lifted me out from the darkness within

Forgiven I was for my doubt and my sin

Letting go of all else in His arms I did rest

Protected, beloved, undoubtedly blest

He is my dear love, my greatest treasure

Joy that exceeds the lure of life's pleasure

Chorus

His lullaby song rings ever so clear

"Hush little one, there is nothing to fear

My love for you grows with each beat of my heart

A love that cannot die nor ever depart

You are precious to me; I love you so

I laid down my life just so you would know

The depth of my love, my mercy my grace

Oh, look at me now, look into my face

And rest, my dear love, rest here in my arms

Forever my strength will keep you from harms

Wherever you go wherever you are

My Glory will shine as your guiding star

When the sorrows of life cause you to roam

My lullaby song will lead you back home"

Yea, doubtless and I count all things but loss for the excellency of the knowledge of Christ Jesus my Lord.

Philippians 3:8

All Else I Count But Loss

Amid the darkest, lonely night

When all my world came tumbling down

Your ray of hope a glimmering light

Reached deep within my soul

To draw me nearer to thy cross

To gaze upon thy face of love

All else, this world I count as loss

Besides thee Lord, my one desire

Body worn from all the years

Of battles fought and battles lost

Despite the life so filled with tears

I find in you my peace, my joy

In Moments filled with guilt and shame

Your Love has held me tight

Never once to point in blame

You gave for me Your life

This world so filled with pain and fear

You are my only hope

I feel your heartbeat drawing near

Held tight within your arms

Your arms provide me strength and might

To face a brand-new day

And cradle me through each dark night

With hymns of wondrous praise

As I gaze back o'er the years

With all their ups and downs

I see the laughter and the tears

That pointed me to You

I thank you Lord, Your guiding hand
Has led me all the way
This life of mine as you had planned
On mountaintops and valleys deep

To draw me nearer to thy cross
To gaze upon thy face of love
All else, this world I count as loss
Besides thee Lord, my one desire

For as the Sufferings of Christ abound in us, so our consolation also aboundeth by Christ

(2 Corinthians 1:5)

Out of the Ashes

I do not understand

Your nail scarred hand

Why you had to bleed

That I might be freed

From the chains of my sin

The darkness within

Can you help me to see?

This great mystery

Why the joy that I sought

With your blood you bought

I am so blinded still

Rebel to Your will

Fool that I am

My life just a sham

To think that my gain

Should come with no pain

So, when trials come

I become glum

As I cry out, "unfair"

Screaming "Are you still there?"

(Bridge)

Then, Gently, so gently you reached out your hand

To cradle me there to help me to stand

Your Love did allow my pain and despair

That I might see You ARE my answered prayer

If I had not walked through the darkest of night

Then, would I have longed for your glorious light

Until I was broken, my life undone

I loved from afar Your Precious Dear Son

There in my darkness Your love drew me in

A humbled and broken heart you did win

And then you unveiled this great mystery

The Love I had sought was inside of me

Out of the ashes to my heart's surprise

A joyous love song began now to rise

From my broken heart

Came a brand-new start

Now I understand

Your nail scarred hand

Helped my eyes to see

That my victory

Was already won

By your precious son

So, whatever the pain

Or torrential rain

In your arms I do hide

In Your love I abide

For You are my pleasure,

My Joy and My treasure

From my broken heart

Came a brand-new start

Helped me understand

Your nail scarred hand

Helped my eyes to see

That my victory

Was already won

By your precious son

So, whatever the pain

Or torrential rain

In your arms I do hide

In Your love I abide

For You are my pleasure,

My Joy and My treasure

The Lord will cross the sea of storms and will calm
its turbulence.

Zechariah 10:11 NET

Anchored

When the storms of life come crashing in
And toss you to and fro
How will you survive? How can you win?
Unless this truth you know
That Christ has won the victory
And Christ can calm the raging sea
In Christ you're anchored by His love
And tethered to His throne above

My dear, dear friend I wish to say

The words you need to help you find

The truth, the life, to never stray

I wish that I were always kind

And never stumbled on this road

Example shined like purest gold

Yet, when I've fallen on my face

God picked me up, for that is Grace

So, dear dear friend I hope you see

That God's dear Son who loved me so

Had paid the price and bought for me

A life of hope now here below

My greatest wish, my one desire

Is that you see the raging fire

A passion for my Lord and King

I pray my life this one song sing

When the storms of life come crashing in
And toss you to and fro
How will you survive? How can you win?
Unless this truth you know
That Christ has won the victory
And Christ can calm the raging sea
In Christ you're anchored by His love
And tethered to His throne above

I wish for you what I have found

For you to know His love

That you might stand on solid ground

Held tight by God Above

I hope you know His love is true

He gave His life to rescue you

So, in this sorrow that you face

I hope you find Amazing Grace

When the storms of life come crashing in
And toss you to and fro
How will you survive? How can you win?
Unless this truth you know
That Christ has won the victory
And Christ can calm the raging sea
In Christ you're anchored by His love
And tethered to His throne above

Now when He (Jesus) got into a boat, His disciples
followed Him. And suddenly a great tempest arose
on the sea, so that the boat was covered with the
waves. But He was asleep. Theni His disciples
came to Him and awoke Him, saying, "lord, save
us! We are perishing!"   But He said to them, "Why
are you fearful, O you of little faith?" Then He
arose and rebuked the winds and the sea, and
there was a great calm. So, the men marveled,
saying, "Who can this be, that even the winds and
the sea obey Him?" Matthew 8: 23-27

Safe
Throughout the Storm

The storm was raging in the night
Our house in certain peril
The lightening flash, the only light
To break the darkest hour

The thunder roar enlarged the fear
The pelting rain and hail
Twas certain now, tornado near
No where were we to run

I felt the arms that held me tight
They carried me to shelter
I felt the strength, the love, the might
My father's arms could give me

His shadow there, the door secure
Though raging winds pulled hard
He did not budge, His mission pure
To keep his children safe

There is safety in his arms
Those arms that hold me tight
So filled with love, so free from harms
It is his love, his gracious love
That keeps me safe throughout the storm

The storm was raging in my life
And darkness filled my heart
My hope was gone, my world was strife
Nowhere to run, depart

I had no strength to stand against
This whirlwind spiraling down
This heart of mine ripped 'way each fence
I knew I neared to drown

And then I felt the arms of love
Enwrap me with His self
I could not feel the winds above
While sheltered in His arms

To think that God would love me so
To cry with each my tear
From there His throne to reach below
And hold me oh so dear

There is safety in His arms
Those arms that hold me tight
So filled with love, so free from harms
It is His love, his gracious love
That keeps me safe throughout the storm

For which cause we faint not; but though our outward man perish, yet the inward man is renewed day by day. For our light affliction, which is but for a moment worketh for us a far more exceeding and eternal weight of glory; While we look not at the things which are see, but at the things which are not seen: for the things which are seen are temporal; but the things which are not seen are eternal. 2 Corinthians 4:16-18

When Loss is Gain

As I look back upon my life
The times of joy and times of strife
How could I cry for any loss?
Once I have gazed upon Thy Cross

How could I ever dare complain?
About life's sorrows, tears and pains
When You so freely took my shame
Upon Yourself removed my blame

Because from sin You set me free
I now thy willing servant be
So, pierce my heart-declare me thine
And purge all selfish thought of mine

If all I have, You choose to take
That Glory bring for your namesake
Allow me gaze upon Thy Face
Thy eyes of love, thy smile of Grace

I do not know what life may bring
Prepare my heart to always sing
A Song of joy, abounding praise
Amidst the billowing storms that raise

For You my precious, Lord and King
Will lift me high on eagle's wing
To soar above this world below
And cast aside the grief and woe

Therefore, you now have sorrow; but I will see you again and your heart will rejoice, and your joy no one will take from you. John 16:22

Because He lives, we can face tomorrow with joy regardless of what may come.

Would I Love You Even More?

I felt the searing, pelting rain

Deep within my soul

I was uncertain where to turn

Or what should be my goal

I gazed upon a cross so far

That stood upon a hill

A Lion strong had died a Lamb

He gave His life at will

That I so undeserving be

Might see His face of love

A Glimpse Glory

His, to fill me from above

Chorus:

Would I love You just the same?

When my life is filled with shame

When pain is all I know

Would my love for You still show?

Can I show Your Glory still?

Accept this sorrow as Your will

When my heart broken in two

Cradled in Your hands, renew

As on Your hope my wings do soar

Would I love You even more?

God's Song of Love

I fell before your precious throne

With broken heart so all alone

My tears were falling like the rain

And then I heard this sweet refrain

Chorus

I have loved you before the dawn of time

Desired to give my joy sublime

My love held tight

By my own might

Come, dear child, I'll hold you near

Wrapped in my love there is no fear

Cradled tight within my arms

Safely kept from this world's harms

I'll sing my song of love for you

Your hope and joy I will renew

Amazed by grace, my hope did grow

Enlightened heart his love doth know

All fear now gone, I rise to run

For I am God's dear precious one

As He sang

Chorus:

I have loved you before the dawn of time

Desired to give my joy sublime

My love held tight

By my own might

Come, dear child, I'll hold you near

Wrapped in my love there is no fear

Cradled tight within my arms

Safely kept from this world's harms

I'll sing my song of love for you

Your hope and joy I will renew

So, as I walk this journey here

I'll love and live without the fear

For I will stand with faith so strong

Because for me He sings this song

Chorus:

I have loved you before the dawn of time

Desired to give my joy sublime

My love held tight

By my own might

Come, dear child, I'll hold you near

Wrapped in my love there is no fear

Cradled tight within my arms

Safely kept from this world's harms

I'll sing my song of love for you

Your hope and joy I will renew

The kingdom of heaven is like unto treasure hid in
a field; the which when a man hath found, he
hideth, and for joy thereof goeth and selleth all
that he hath, and buyeth that field. Matthew 13:44

Your Treasure is Already Here

In the dark of the night
In the midst of a dream
When shadows surround
The heart wants to scream
Of sorrows and pains
The guilt that constrains
Eyes open to search for light's beam

Then a whisper, s song
God's truth in a thought
His promise of love
Salvation He bought
The fears of the night
Must now take their flight
As He is the Joy, I have sought

In the dark of the night
In the midst of man's scheme
Christ whispered my name
His prayer bore this theme
To give me His love
His joy from above
This wretch he did so esteem

And so "Heart do not cry!
And mind do not fear!"
Your God hath a plan
To bring your heart cheer
You may not see now
The way or the how
Yet, your treasure is already here

When my spirit was overwhelmed within me, then thou knewest my path Psalm 142:3

Why word is a lamp unto my fee, and a light unto my path. Psalm 119:105

Journey Through This Rugged Land

As I gaze back over my years
The wretched scars, rivers of tears
This journey long through rocky land
That all of this, all as You planned

For in the midst of sorrows here
I heard Your voice as You drew near
The Joy I sought from all these things
This world could give, had taken wings

When all was gone and all seemed loss
I saw Your Son upon that cross
His Love reached forth to rescue me
My selfish Heart He did set free

'Twas there I came to realize
That with all lost, to my surprise
My Joy was now a flowing stream
More wondrous than my greatest dream

Love now filled this heart of mine
My heart enwrapped with Love Divine
And now I knew this pain took place
That I might learn of Your Sweet Grace

My Sorrows, pain You did allow
That I vain joys would disavow
This joy I know; this love I feel
Your Love, Your Joy You did reveal

Amidst my bitter pain and tears
You held my hand through all the years
You never let me slip away
Steady beside me you did stay

Patient, gentle with heart so kind
You waited, watched for me to find
You are the treasure I did seek
Your gentle kiss upon my cheek

Reminds me that You will my best

And on this promise, I can rest

My journey long through rugged land

Has been the one True Love had planned

For in Him we live, and move, and have our being
(Acts 17:28)

For all things in heave and on earth were created in
Him—all things, whether visible or invisible,
whether thrones or dominions, whether
principalities or powers—all things were created
through Him and for Him. He Himself is before all
things and all things are held together in Him.

(Colossians 1:16-17)

Out of the Nothingness

When I look in the mirror to gaze at my face
The scars deep within I cannot erase
The years that I tried to stand on my own
Wanting to be and to be known

I tried, oh so hard to do what was right
To struggle with all my strength and my might
Falling so short, I never could be
More than the darkness deep inside me

There where I saw the truth of my plight
Nothing in me could ever bring light
Into the darkness that shone all around
No hope to conquer as evils abound

Then when I knew there was nothing in me
That could calm the raging, roaring sea
You were the one who reached out Your hand
Showing me how in You I could stand

My LORD and King in Sovereignty Reign

Washing me clean of my guilty stain

That out of the nothingness that is me

You enter in that I might then be

The warrior You need to go to the fight

Telling the world of Your strength and might

While singing a song of joyous delight

Shining with truth in your glorious light

When I can see the world through your eyes

Trusting in You to make my heart wise

I become Nothing, that You then can be

The bright shining hope for the world to see

That out of the nothingness that is me

You enter in that I might then BE

For all the promises of God in Him are yea, and in Him Amen, unto the glory of God by us 2 Corinthians 1:20.

Your Promises Are Always True

This journey filled with sometimes pain

The storms, with dark incessant rain

A fleeting moment of sunshine

Reminds me of Your Truth Divine

That You, dear Lord, are by my side

And that in You, I can abide

So, oft; dear Lord I cannot see

The truth of how Your guiding me

When evil lurks, to bring me down

Attempting in its darkness drown

The fact that You have won this war

That Safely I will reach the shore

My safety is not based on me

My life was bought on Calvary

It was there you reached your hand of Grace

And there my sins You did erase

The truth of You, who drew me near

Is why this life I do not fear

Your promises are always true

That every path you lead me through

Will bring me joy, a hope above

That draws me closer to your love

So, when I do not understand

I'll trust Your word that guides Your hand

For thou art my lamp, O Lord: and the Lord will
lighten my darkness

2 Samuel 22:29

What Do You Do in the Dark of the Night?

What do you do in the dark of the night?
When all of your dreams, the hopes you held tight
Came crashing down, your world shattered, profound!
Heartbreaking tears, oh the wretched sound!
Can faith hold firm when hope is lost from sight?

It wasn't the answer that my heart did long
I find it so hard to sing a praise song
When all that my heart did once long for, desire
Scattered as ashes by Your raging fire
Was it my fault, Lord, had I been so wrong?

Yet, if I look back, my story be told
Through gleeful spring days, and winters so cold
In the center of all, it has always been You
Who never let go, my Love to pursue
Your Glory, Your Grace; Your strength took ahold

How many years of sorrow, you've borne
While we shout Your name, and blame you with scorn
Your patience and Grace that brings each new day
While waiting for us to see You're the way
Through Jesus Your son, our spirit reborn

When I consider Your Love from the start
That sent forth your Son, His throne to depart
To die on a cross, forsaken, forlorn
Facing such shame, disgrace, and such scorn
To Justly His Righteousness to Impart

On someone like me, so ravaged with pride
Who of my free will would never decide
To follow the one who loved me so true
That down crooked paths my love to pursue
Calling me there to walk by Your side

So,

What do I do in the dark of the night?

I run to seek You, my one guiding light

To sit in your presence, ever so still

Until I'm conformed, whatever Your will

To follow with faith, regardless of sight

Along the Road of Life

As I walked along this road of life
Amidst the rambling thorns of strife
I felt the pains-like sharpened knife
Tear open scars of yonder day

I gazed before me - looming there
Mountains filled with evil lair
I wanted then to cry a prayer
Yet, sorrow's silence stole my way

I felt so desperately alone
Until a light before me shone
A King who sat upon a throne
A path to whom before me lay

And then I heard a still small voice
That called to me to sing, rejoice
I pondered then to make the choice
To choose Joy's song as mine today

I felt within a warmth, a glow

It felt as if my heart did grow

As joy and love within did flow

My pains and sorrows swept away

I took a step, just one at first

Desiring more His hope I thirst

To drink His love until I burst

With laughter's wondrous ray

My heart rejoicing rose to sing

As lifted high on eagle's wing

My weakness bids- His strength to bring

My fears and doubts He came to slay

Amazing then before my eyes

The mountains that had hid the skies

No longer did before me rise

Instead beneath my feet did lay

Family & friends

115

Choose you this day whom ye will serve; whether the gods which your fathers served that were on the other side of the flood, or the gods of the Amorites, in whose land ye dwell; but as for me and my house, we will serve the Lord. Joshua 24:15

All These Years

I thank you Lord for all these years
For every laugh and even tears
Your Wondrous Grace has led the way
And pulled me close when I did stray
My life has truly been so blessed
Your joy, Your hope, Your love possessed
This heart of mine-You have held me tight
Through sun kissed days and dark of night
What wondrous gifts you have given me
The love and joy of family
What mercy, grace on me did shine
You chose these children to be mine
What wondrous smile upon Your face!
To gift me with such love and grace!!
Beyond all this You then did send
Each precious one that I call friend
Like angels on this earth to guide
Friends in which I can confide
One truth in which I must attest
You have given me Your best

117

I thank you Lord for all You have done

But most of all for your dear Son

Who gave His all to ransom me!

That blessed I am eternally

Lo, children are a heritage of the Lord: and the
fruit of the womb is His reward. Psalm 127:3

God's Blessing to Me, My Children Three

I asked the Lord so long ago
To bless my soul, I didn't know
He'd take me down to depths so low
Before I saw which way to go

His gift He gave in bundles three
That brought me tears and brought me glee
Each pain they felt a knife ripped me
So oft I fell on bended knee

Nearer now to setting sun
I see the truth of what He's done
My daughter dear and my two sons
A gift of perfect love I'd won

Melissa, dear – a sweet sweet flower
Who serves with love – whatever hour
With gracious smile her love does shower
A hope to each- to them empower

Alberto with bewitching smile
Bubbling joy, he doth beguile
The world around to stay a while
To learn of Honor, Truth—his style

And Ron, my precious son doth stand
With justice, truth held in his hand
With mercy, love he doth command
A tower strong the winds withstand

So, as I looked upon these three
No greater gift could ever be
Such perfect love God gave to me
With thankful heart I shout with glee

He answered thus my soul's great plea
He blessed me with these wondrous three
His Glory to shine for me to see
Their lives reflecting Him to me.

For I know the thoughts that I think toward you,
saith the Lord, thoughts of peace, and not of evil,
to give you an expected end. Then shall ye call
upon me, and ye shall go and pray unto me, and I
will hearken unto you. And ye shall seek me, and
find me, when ye shall search for me with all your
heart And I will be found of you saith the Lord: and
I will turn away your captivity. Jeremiah 29: 11-14

Some Would Say I am Lucky

Some would say I am lucky
Some would say achieved
Yet, Lord I know the truth to be
It was an act of your pure grace
That Showered down on me

A little girl with doll in hand
You chose and called her name
To follow you, the life you planned
With glee, she quickly came

She dreamed of love, the perfect life
With children running round
White picket fence and never strife
Where joy it must abound

In eagerness she ran ahead
And could not see the peril
She wanted just to please, instead
She donned her guilt apparel

Amidst the dark and treacherous path
She feared God's love had gone
Each trial seen, she thought was wrath
For all that she had done.

A ray of glorious hope shone down
As in her arms God laid each child
And on each child He placed His crown
God's gift of love so gentle, mild

And then I looked back o'er the years
And realized it was God's Grace
That lead me through so many tears
That I might see His face

I see my children fully grown
Their babies in their arms
I marvel at the grace you've shone
Their life displays your charms

My treasure Lord, in you I've found
My storms of heart you calm
Your gifts of grace overflowing round
Your precious saints that call me "MOM"

Some would say I am lucky
Some would say achieved
Yet, Lord I know the truth to be
It was an act of your pure grace
That Showered down on me

Many daughters have done virtuously, but thou
excellest them all. Proverbs 31:29

My Little Girl

My little girl I see you now
Your baby in your arms
It takes me back to years ago
To you with all your charms

I loved you so my precious sweet
I'd give the world for you
Yet life it turned and choices made
I thought were best for you

I thought I didn't have enough
To give my little girl
To keep you safe, to give you more
I sacrificed my world

I prayed each day God keep you safe
Beneath His wings of love
That all life's pain and grief
He'd help you soar above

And yet, my love, I see you now
This mother you've become
I know that God answered my prayer
With joy, I'm overcome

I love you so, my precious one
Though womanhood you've found
You'll always be my little girl
Though years keep turning round

The greatest gift I give to you
Is Jesus Christ, God's son
Who paid the price, that hand in hand
Equipping you this race to run

So rest within this perfect truth
He has the perfect plan
For you and now your little girl
He cradles in His hand

Children's children are the crown of old men; and
the glory of children are their fathers.

Proverbs 17:6

Natalie's Song

The twinkle in her deep brown eyes
The smile that lights her face
Her words at times so deep and wise
With gentle touch of grace

She laughs and plays with awe struck joy
The wonder life does bring
With Emmy, Sophie or a toy
Her heart with joy does sing

You blessed her Lord with Mom and Dad
A special pair indeed
Safely in their love she's clad
While gently they do lead

As I bow my head today
To seek your presence, Lord
I ask you guide her heart to say
"God is my true reward"

CHORUS:

That her light shine bright

In the dark of the night

Let her song sing forth to the world

With a joy filled glee

Your glory to see

In the heart of this little girl

Lord I ask you guide her steps

As only you can do

When journeys lead to valleys depth

Or mountains come in view

Hold her in your loving arms

To wipe away each tear

Protecting her from all life's harms

And drive away each fear

Let your joy so fill her heart

With love for your dear son

Through faith and hope that you impart

Her victory has been won

CHORUS:

Lord, I ask for one more thing:

That her light shine bright

In the dark of the night

Let her song sing forth to the world

With a joy filled glee

Your glory to see

In the heart of this little girl

My Dear Precious Girls
A Tribute to Annabella Grace and Clara Noelle Barba

I thought of my dear precious girls

With spiky hair or bouncy curls

How do they make my heart so light!

Memories of joy and pure delight

Ever Close within my heart

God's Grace to me He did impart

To let me spend these years so near

The laughter, joys and even the tears

My precious dancer, Annabella Grace

Passionate princess with sparkling face

Ablaze with fantasy would say

Grammy, Grammy let's go and play

Each game she would craft with minute detail

My part designed so I could not fail

Then Clara Noelle, a heart full of joy

Who laughed, and smiled or sometimes be coy

Her strength and endurance rising above

To conquer life trials by her enduring love

Although for now I live so far away

I think of you both and this I do pray,

"O Father dear let each child know

The depth of love I long to bestow

Yet, more important, let them do see

Your love for them, to be their glee

Fill their hearts with love for you Dear Lord

Teach them You are their greatest reward

You are the hope the joy their heart desires

The wisdom and strength life's journey requires

And let them know that You are the One

Who gave to them your Precious Son

That in Him their life will always be

Overflowing with love and victory.

Awaken Now for Your Birthday
Gabriela Faith Barba

God did touch your heart and say

Come forth, my child come forth today

Your life 'til now formed you to be

A Wondrous mirror reflecting me

My Grace and Love that gave you life

Will be there through this world of strife

Remember child, I'll always be

One breath, one prayer away-you see

I have a plan based on my grace

To bring you close to see my face

For now, I've asked your Mom and Dad

To be the ones to make you glad

Providing all that you will need

To grow in Grace and to succeed

Becoming all that I have planned

The perfect life I so designed

That you might reach and take my hand

One day before my throne to stand

The life I gave you months ago

I placed within your Mom to grow

140

It is time to leave where you did stay

Awaken now for your Birthday

142

Haley's World

Meow, Hiss, roar
I heard her say
Woof, Woof, GRRR
Imagination at play

She looks at life
With simplicity
The trials that come
She shrieks with a plea

Daddy, I miss you
You are the one
I want to be near
From early morn to setting sun

Wearing her heart
So, open you see
With passion she cries
Or laughs heartily

Never the one to
Think for a while
Before she responds
With a tear or a smile

A lizard or worm
Can bring her such joy
Perhaps even more
Than her dinosaur toy

But one day so quick
She will grow up and find
The world is not always
So pure or so kind

Or maybe it is
She already does know
So, meow, grr, roar
Is her way to show

That life is not fair
It can be so tough
So filled with the pains
Of everyday stuff

So, this is my prayer
That Father you will
Guide her dear path
And teach her Your skill

How joy can be found
By trusting in You
Whatever may come
Your love is so true

You are the one
Who knows her dear heart!
And You are the one who
Will never depart.

How excellent is thy lovingkindness, O God!
Therefore, the children of men put their trust under
the shadow of thy wings. Psalm 36:7

When Grammy Must Go

Ode to Aiden

Grammy, Grammy you are here!

I heard his little voice

And saw his grin from ear to ear

To love had been his choice

As I looked into that face

That filled my life with joy

My grandson stood there in this place

This little precious boy

(Bridge 1)

So why must I go Lord

And leave this precious child

With Broken heart

I must depart

At your command I go

Lord, I know your plan is best

The years have taught me this

Upon your love, my soul doth rest

Although his smile I'll miss

Now dear Lord, then show me how

To say that I must leave

In such a way, my love doth show

And he's not left to grieve

(Bridge 2)

Let your love pour down, Lord

Surround his heart with you

Fill him with joy

This dear little boy

Full of hope, and joy, and love

And now I must go

Lay aside all this woe

For you, my precious King

Will take care of everything

Love is patient, love is kind, it is not envious. Love does not brag; it is not puffed up. It is not rude, it is not self-serving, it is not easily angered or resentful. It is not glad about injustice but rejoices in the truth. It bears all things, believes all things, hopes all things, endures all things. Love never ends. I Corinthians 13:4-8

A Broken Vessel's Vow

Two hearts had joined as one that day

And never saw the dark pathway

That lay ahead and lay behind

Two hearts that joined in hope to find

A strength in love to shine a light

Upon their lonely darkest night

Each had brought with them their fears

Their brokenness and all their tears

And as their story did unfold

Two broken hearts their sorrow told

It was not what they hoped that day

Can broken hearts still find a way?

A miracle is what they'd need

If ever they were to succeed

God's gracious love must touch a heart

To help them stay, to not depart

Two broken hearts can beat as one

Because of Grace from God's own son

The broken hearts are me and you

I ran to hide, to bid adieu

And then I saw your tear stained face

My heart was filled with love and grace

I saw the beauty of your heart

The tenderness you could impart

A brilliant mind so trapped within

I saw the man you could have been

If only you had known God's love

His strength could help you rise above

And so I vow to love you dear

Today and through each passing year

My strength must come from God alone

As now I bow before His throne

I will lay aside all my desire

That God might flame my passion fire

To rise within to find the strength

That I might go the final length

To love you better stronger still

For this I know has been God's will

Pedro Barba, Jr. 1/15/1942-7/23/1994

A Transcendent Love

I searched for love that would transcend
The spans of time, to never end
To find someone to call my own
And carry me to heights unknown
Of joyous hope, a dearest friend

Love's mystery is so profound
The sea of tears in which I have drowned
To turn to search for love again
Believing that I could begin
From losing you, I could rebound

And as the years, the time went by
Sometimes, I still would start to cry
A song, a word that brought to mind
My love for you, my heart resigned
Your gentle kiss, your last goodbye

Love truly is a mystery
A part of you remains with me
Although you left me long ago
And left this journey here below
You live within my memory

And so, I found that deep within
A greater love was mine to win
It was God's love there all along
That taught to me a true love song
A life of joy and hope begin

Oh, what a wondrous song of Grace
That love should be His Glorious face
That broken hearts should find Him there
With eyes of love so gentle, fair
His arms reach forth our hearts embrace

That through our pain, we come to view
The depth of love when love is true
The patient, gentle voice of love
That bid Him from His throne above
To bear a cross for me and you

Although you left me long ago
And I still walk this earth below
I've found the love that I did seek
Though of His love you did not speak
You taught me the truth that I must know

You taught my blinded eyes to see
The depth of love God had for me
I had thought that I was there for you
To teach God's love for you to view
My sorrow brought humility

There in your broken world of fear
You reached in love to draw me near
I see it now, it was God's Grace
That brought us both to seek His face
Through rivers built upon a tear

I found a love that would transcend
The spans of time, to never end
I found someone to call my own
And carry me to heights unknown
Of joyous hope, a dearest friend

Death Cannot Hold My Heart in Pain

I felt the breeze across my face
Like gentle kiss of grace
I heard the warbling birds that sing
Now calling forth the spring

The winter ice cut deep my bone
With Screams you are alone
You left me one mid summer's day
To ne'er return my way

Oh death, how could you take my love?
To be with God above
While leaving me upon this earth
Amidst its wanton dearth

Ah, but now this gentle breeze of spring
A hope on which to cling
It is God's Grace that loves me so
To now bid me to know

That I might laugh and dance once more

As I had done before

To know that love is mine within

Christ did the victory win

Death cannot hold my heart in pain

When God doth joy sustain

This ache, this sorrow will be gone

And bring a brand new dawn

My Love, I must bid thee adieu

Until we meet anew

For now, I must live on my dear

A life not built on fear

To find the joy of Christ in me

Abundant life to see

That I am loved beyond measure

For God is my treasure

Fear not; for thou shalt not be ashamed: neither be thou confounded; for thou shalt not be put to shame: for thou shalt forget the shame of thy youth, and shalt not remember the reproach of thy widowhood any more. For thy Maker is thine husband; the Lord of hosts is his name; and thy Redeemer the Holy One of Israel; The god of the whole earth shall He be called. Isaiah 54:4-5

Johnnie Gray Garner---Mom. 12/12/1930-6/29/2020

I Was A Child, Back Then

I was a child, back then
And did not, could not understand
The pains she faced, the fears within
Her road of life throughout this land

But as I grew I came to see
The sacrifices that she made
Because of love she had for me
No matter what it did not fade

Whatever road our feet did trod
Her courage, faith deep within
Did hold her heart close to God
Protecting her from sin

The more I learned of God's dear Grace
Throughout the years, I came to see
The trials, sorrows that we face
Transform our hearts that we might be

A shining beacon on a hill
To light the path in darkest night
That strangers then might find God's will
The blinded might gain sight

Yet, each of us, God calls to be
A different beam of Glory's light
And this in part the mystery
Of how God works, that He just might

Give one the gift to speak His word
Another sings His praise
While some it seems their voice unheard
Except by God. In prayer their voices raise

Each child who knows Christ as their Lord
God uses in His own sweet way
To each He gives a different sword
His Glory Honor to display

And so, I came to realize
The chains of pride that bound my heart
Were merely part of Satan's guise
Sow bitter seeds, and then depart

I lay my "self" upon the cross
The cross where Jesus bled and died
That He might live, all else is loss
My pride He's crucified

As I look back, I now can see
That it was Mom, God used to be
A beacon of humility
His beam of Grace to shine toward me

I did not, could not understand
The pains she faced, the fears within
Her road of life throughout this land
Because I was a child, back then

Certainly, you made my mind and heart; you wove
me together in my mother's womb. Your eyes saw
me when I was inside the womb. All the days
ordained for me were recorded in Your scroll before
one of them came into existence. How difficult it is
for me to fathom Your thoughts about me, O God!
Psalm 139: 13,16-17 (NET)

To Mom: It Seems Like Yesterday

It seems like only Yesterday
You watched over us as we did play
The time has flown throughout the years
With times of laughter and of tears
At times I did not understand
Yet, it has been as God planned
You always taught me to say
"He knows what's best, so let us pray"
It was your faith that stood so strong
Teaching me In Christ I do belong
To lean on Him through each dark day
And never, ever fail to pray
Or raise our voices loud to sing
For He is Lord and He is King
At times, the laughter filled our home
And followed us wherever we roamed
There were the times of happiness
Where joy and peace brought their rest
Then, through the years as Mom and friend
You have always been there to the end
You picked me up each time I fell

And taught me in God's Grace to dwell.

No matter what when I did stray

You would warn me harsh, but you did stay.

Right by my side to help me stand

Obedience to each command

I learned through trials I did face

While you stood near to show me grace

Your love for me unparalleled

To those I desired which were dispelled

Into the bleakest, darkest night

So far from joy, so far from sight

And when my heart broke with despair

You were the one, you were there

To pick me up, to hear my cries

And then to dry my tear stained eyes

You were there whenever I called

You came so quick and never stalled

To help me raise my children dear

You were here and always near

Throughout the years I watched your pain

Yet through it all, your faith remain!

Therefore, I want to scream unfair

You confused weak, with frightened stare

"Why, dear Lord, must she face this

After a life devoid of bliss

Dear God, I do not know today

The words of which I should pray

So, I must fall before thy throne

And ask that she not feel alone

That you may wrap her in your arms

Protecting her through all life's harms

I have learned, my Lord that through the pains

The sorrows and torrential rains

You draw us nearer to your side

That in Your love we may abide

And though I may not understand

Upon Your Grace, my faith doth stand

I know that Mom is in Your Will

So, on that truth I will stand still.

For we walk by faith, not by sight: We are
confident, I say, and willing rather to be absent
from the body, and to be present with the Lord.
(2 Corinthians 5:7-9)

Set Free Today (6/29/2020)

Mom's spirit was set free today

To see her Lord, while I did pray

I know she could not wait for me

To join her in her jubilee

But one day there will a trumpet sound

When joyously my heart will pound

So if He calls me home before

Or on that day, for evermore

I too shall see Him face to face

Because of His Unending Grace

So, dry my tears, how can I cry?

Into God's arms my mom did fly

Where joy abounds

And Love Surrounds

God's Glory does forever shine

The peace of God today is mine

I know where mom has gone today

She always knew and showed the way

I will miss you Mom, my dearest friend

Your faith shone forth unto the end

To My Son, Ron

I cried out to God
That early morn
To touch your life
As you were born

Into a world of evil pain

I prayed for Him

To there remain

Ever close within your heart

By His bright light

Show you the way

And when the time

Teach you to pray

That through the darkness

Of this world

Upon your life

His grace be hurled

So, tiny fragile

There you were

Just 4 pounds

So Premature

And yet the man
You grew to be
So, filled with strength
And bravery

A heart of gold
That fills your chest
To help you rise
Above the rest

With Honor, justice
Your decree
As black and white
The world you see

While striving hard
To do what's right
With all your strength
And all your might

174

I see your heart

Its depth of love

The struggles great

You have soared above

God's love for you

It Knows no bounds

The depth and width

And height resounds

Nothing on earth

Can separate

Your life from

His determined fate

So, when your life

Is filled with strife

It merely is

His surgeon's knife

Then you Shall see,
my dear son
When God's transforming
Work is done

That He transformed
Both heart and soul
To look like Christ
His One True goal

And then when looking
Back you'll see
The pains and sorrows
Lead to glee

The only joy that's
Really real
The one that nothing
Else can steal

Is found in Him
Who loves you so
He Gave Himself
That you might know

The height, the depth,
The width of love
He pours on you
From up above

And when you see
His Glorious face
In awe of His
Amazing Grace

You will understand
All that He has done
Because He loved
You Dear, my Son

To Alberto with Love

It was 5 in the evening
On that fate filled day
God answered a prayer
I ne'er knew to pray

As into my world
Of sorrow and pain
God sent me a son
Who would break the chain

Life was not easy
For him or for me
But somehow, he found
A way to bring glee

The trials they came
And life seemed so hard
At times both our hearts
And spirits were charred

By the flames of this world
The evil around
Despite which God's joy
Did always abound

For God only knew
The man he would be
After life's trials
Had turned him to see

That God is the one
Who created his life
And God had allowed
The sorrows and strife

That he would become
A man who loved God

Who could bring joy and hope
Wherever he trod

And so, my dear son
On this your birthday
Just give me a moment
For this to say

So proud I am son
Of the man you have become
Reflecting the attributes
Of Jesus, God's son

Not always perfect
As you will be one day
But upright and true
You follow The Way

It was 5 in the evening
On that fate filled day
God answered a prayer
I Ne'er knew to pray

Friends

A Friend loveth (always), and a brother is born for adversity (to be there for you in times of need).

Proverbs 17:16-18

GOD'S GIFT OF A FRIEND

So precious the gift when God gives you a friend
To lift you, to guide you, to cheer to the end
Like Angels of hope when skies turn to gray
They know where you've been, and they choose to stay

When sorrows would try to invade for a while
They know the right words to make your heart smile
They have taken the time to know who you are
Beneath all the pain, beneath all the scar

They know who you are and who you can be
And know the right words to set your heart free
They shine in your life like beacons of light
That ward off the fear and the darkness of night

When fiery trials of life must come your way
They know what to do and know what to say
They reach forth their hand and quench all the flame
While joyously laugh, "all is well" they proclaim

They enter our lives like a whisper, a prayer

We never do know just how long they'll be there

Yet, so precious a gift of God's love and His grace

Is shown in their eyes and shown in their face

You never do know what tomorrow may bring

So today is the day to dance and to sing

Their journey may lead them to far, far away

So cherish this moment and cherish this day

God Sends You a Note

God sends you a note

Though someone else wrote

A text or a rhyme or a quote

And through what was said

A hope fills your head

As down some path you felt lead

Joy fills your heart

And flames with a spark

Like a dream, a beginning, a start

Then something goes wrong

Like some sad country song

And you feel like you just don't belong

Then you lift up your eyes

Filled with tears toward the skies

And you ask God to please tell you why

While tears fall like rain

And your heart breaks with pain

Your sorrow no truth can explain

It had nothing to do

With the one before you

As the truth your dear heart doth pursue

God saw deep within

Saw the scars held therein

Left behind from the past where you'd been

So God sent you this oar

To help find the shore

And to force you to unlock that door

So the wound could now heal

And that burden so real

Could be crushed so that now you might feel

The release from that chain

That had caused so much strain

So, God's joy and His Glory might reign

AMERICA

189

.

Blessed is the nation whose God is the Lord; and
the people whom He hath chosen for His own
inheritance. Psalm 33:12

United, The Land of the Free

Anger and hate, division, and strife

Filling the streets, choking out life

How do we, Lord, know what really is true?

When lies, hate and fear are all that they spew

They scream they want love, that all should unite

By disruption, destruction all through the night

The media lies, the elitists do cheer

Controlling the mobs with hate and with fear

The Power they want, held tight in their hand

If division remains in the heart of the land

How can they not see, how can they not know?

That You are the hope for we creatures below.

By Grace You have stretched out Your loving hand

To the broken, forgotten, each lost soul of this land

You bid them to come and rest in Your peace

Where anger, division, and fear all will cease

To trust in Your love and to Rest in Your Grace

Whatever their background, their creed or their race

You are the one who can set their heart free

Open their eyes that they might then see

That love can be found deep in each heart

When anger and fear has been bid to depart

By Your gift of salvation, bought by Your Son

In Whom we are woven United each one

A Nation of hope for the world all to see

The Truth of the Words "The land of the free"

Symbols of Freedom For All To View

Grammy, Grammy please tell me why
We fly a flag on the fourth of July!

Oh, sweet dear child, the flag you see
Is a symbol of hope; because, we are free
To passionately work with all our might
Transforming our dreams into full sight

It's more than a symbol of national pride
It reflects all those who fought and who died
Protecting our freedom from tyrants who might
Destroy and steal all that is right

Grammy, then please can you tell me why?
We fly a flag on the fourth of July
And don't fly a flag every day of the year
Wouldn't our freedom be something to cheer?

Grammy, Grammy why do people say
We worship the cross on Easter day?

Oh, my dear child, the cross you see
Is a symbol that Jesus has set us free!
Jesus died on a cross to pay for my sin
Then on the third day, He rose again

Jesus loved us so much, He paid our price
For all the times in life that we aren't so nice
He offers to give us a heart that is new
Filled with love, joy and hope for all to view

If only we ask Him into our heart
He promises that He'll never depart
Walking and talking, right by our side
So, that in His presence we might abide

Grammy, then why do people say
We worship the cross on Easter Day?
Would not we worship God everyday
Singing Him praise, and bowing to pray?

194

Grammy, I think, since all this is true

Wouldn't our faith then change our view?

Wouldn't we want to help men to see?

That they too by faith, can then be set free?

The flag is a symbol that I can be free

To worship God who helps me to be

The best, the greatest version of me

To be then a light for the world to see

So, to the cross I bow on my knee

By faith I am saved, I am set free

From the chains that would bind

And the lies that would blind

Then, I will stand, saluting the flag

Its symbol of freedom, from age to age

May God bless and guide our nation today

A symbol of hope, for this I pray.

The Lord our God is one Lord:

And thou shalt love the Lord thy God with all thine heart, and with all thy soul, and with all thy might. And these words, which I command thee this day, shall be in thine heart: And thou shalt teach them diligently unto thy children, and shalt talk of them when thou sittest in thine house, and when thou walkest by the way, and when thou liest down and when thou risest up.

American School

A deafening silence fills the halls

As light then fades and darkness falls

A sudden scream, a wailing sound

Where are you God? You cannot be found

The desperate cries, unending tears

From hearts so filled with pain and fears

Angry cries scream forth to blame

And never see the truth, the shame

Dear God, why do not you answer please

To bring your love, our hearts to ease

And then I heard a soft, strong voice

My dearest one, I gave you choice

You cast Me out and shut the door

My Word to read there nevermore

You locked me out of every school

To never teach the Golden rule

No prayer can e'er be spoke aloud
By rich or poor, the meek, the proud
As evil grows within each heart
Because you bid my love depart

You cast me far as you could see
Because my love had set you free
To choose my truth or cast away
Accepting lies that others say

Without my righteous Holy light
There's only darkness of the night
I will not force my way within
Yet, stand without and bid you When?

When will you open up your door?
To let me in forevermore
That I might fill your hearts with peace
And cause the pains and fears to cease

I love you more than you can know
If only you would let me show
To you the love and joy that's mine
Into your darkness let me shine

I am the love and hope you need
That is why I still do plead
That you may turn to seek my face
So, I might pour on you my Grace

I'll write my truth upon your heart
That you might ne'er again depart
And in my joy and love abide
As I walk there at your side

When will you open up your door?
To let me in forevermore
That I might fill your hearts with peace
And cause the pains and fears to cease

When Terror Strikes

When terror strikes from every side
Inciting fear in every heart
When all I see is torn apart
How can I Lord in You abide?
And rest in peace upon they word
With all the hate and sorrow heard
From wretched men, so filled with pride
I need a place in which to hide

I turn and lift my eyes toward You
To search the dark, to understand
How can this be as You have planned?
When all the world seems so askew
By evil hearts so filled with sin
It's hard to see Your love will win
When selfish hearts themselves pursue
Destruction, death and pain ensue

As I gazed there shone forth a light

And reaching forth a steady hand

That held at bay hell's death command

With sovereign power and such might

It is Grace alone that bids you wait

While justice bids man's final fate

That one more broken heart contrite

With blinded eyes to then find sight

Oh, Lord, please help me understand

That the same love that bore the cross

Is Your love for us when we face loss

That Grace holds firm Your Mighty hand

That every kindness we have known

Is proof Your grace for us is shown

For Justice would itself demand

That darkness, death consume our land

So, help me Lord to be a light

To spread your word where e'er I go

Your love, your hope, your joy to show

Your gospel truth to then take flight

Transforming hearts that one by one

They seek and find your precious son

That then your Glory shine so bright

Beams of Grace in the dark of night

If my people which are called by my name shall
humble themselves, and pray, and seek my face,
and turn from their wicked ways; then will I hear
from heaven and will forgive their sin, and will heal
their land 2 Chronicles 7:14

A Prayer OF Healing for Our Land

God of heaven on your throne

Oh, hear our humble cry

And do not leave us here alone

Far from your watchful eye

Though we in selfish pride pursued

Vain Idols of our own

And yet, we know Your Gracious heart

In covenant does stand

That if we now from sin depart

That You will heal our land

Together then our hearts renewed

Rejoice, a brand, new start

So, break our hearts to what breaks yours

Open our eyes to see

The bitter words our mouth outpours

The pride that lies in me

So, dark and looming does occlude

The hope that love restores

So, Lord repentant here we stand

Seeking forgiveness now

Adhere to Your command

Oh, Lord please show us how!

A Cross displayed, Your Grace we viewed

So, let us be your hand

To reach across the great divides

That separate our hearts

To rise one voice devoid of sides

Your love and grace imparts

Your hope and joy, a new prelude

On which our life abides

Freedom's Cry to be Free

Oh, Lord restore law in our land
Those who protect might take a stand
Transform, Dear God, these hearts that hate
Before destruction is our fate

Freedom can't be freedom, until our hearts are free
From all the hate and bigotry
That pride has brought to be
Our eyes so blinded, we can't see
That hate breeds hate inside of me
Our only hope to be set free
You purchased there on Calvary

Oh, Righteous Lord, I hear your cry
Our wayward hearts have made you sigh
Your justice soon, it must draw nigh
Unless repentant we reply

207

Before thy throne we seek your Grace

And Gaze there on your holy Face

Where there our sins you will erase

Our hearts might then your love embrace

To spread to all we meet each day

With humble hearts, we then might say

Come sinner, come to find your way

Here at this altar let us pray

Freedom can't be freedom, until our hearts are free

From all the hate and bigotry

That pride has brought to be

Our eyes so blinded, we can't see

That hate breeds hate inside of me

Our only hope to be set free

You purchased there on Calvary

Oh, Lord bring love within our heart

A love that bids all hate depart

Give this our land a fresh new start

Let each of us now do our part

And Lord, each day by setting sun

Let me not then my duty shun

Reach out my hand to touch someone

To help them see your Precious Son

Freedom can't be freedom, until our hearts are free

From all the hate and bigotry

That pride has brought to be

Our eyes so blinded, we can't see

That hate breeds hate inside of me

Our only hope to be set free

You purchased there on Calvary

If you abide in My Word, you are My disciples indeed. And you shall know the truth, and the truth shall make you free. John 8:31-32 (NKJV)

A Desperate Cry for Truth

I felt the anguish cutting deep
It pierced my heart and soul
The tossing, turning restless sleep
Was taking now it's toll

The lies, corruption circling around
This country once was free
Now chained, the evil words abound
The truth we cannot see

Complacent to be so correct
In silence I had stood
My Christian duty did neglect
I hid beneath this hood

Oh wretched heart, I was to blame
Allowing this to be
Now buried in my sinful shame
I turned to look to Thee

Oh, Lord, please come and hear my cry
I fall here at your feet
As darkness draws, the end is nigh
I must not accept defeat

I heard Your voice, "stand up my child
Together we shall fight
Our spirits, hearts are reconciled
Your sin cast far from sight"

Arise in Grace, my precious one
The truth I have revealed
In Jesus Christ my precious Son
In Him your heart is sealed

I hear the cries for your dear land

So, trust me when I say

Revival is what I'll command

And Truth shall find its way

Behold the Lord's hand is not shortened that it cannot save; nor is His ear heavy that He cannot hear. But your iniquities have separated you from your God; And your sins have hidden His face from you, So that He will not hear. For your hands are defiled with blood, and your fingers with iniquity; Your lips have spoken lies, Your tongue has muttered perversity. No one calls for justice, Nor does any plead for truth. They trust in empty words and speak lies; they conceive evil and bring forth iniquity. Isaiah 59:1-4 (NKJV)

But for God

I see the sorrows that abound
The depths of pain that do surround
Anger, hate the awful sound
Dear Lord, where are you now?
I need to feel you close somehow
To know this pain, you did allow
Help my eyes to just see You
I need somehow to have your view
To see the victory was won
Upon that cross by your dear Son

For there upon a hill so high
A cross that reached into the sky
Your Son did bleed, and He did die
To save a sinner such as I
Oh, Father dear did you cry?
Were there tears that filled your eye?
As you gazed from up above
Steadied your hand, because of love
You saw beyond the wretched pain
And focused then upon the gain

For human hearts so filled with pride
Desire to rule and cast aside
Their only hope, their one true guide
As evil grows within each heart
They grasp it tight, to ne'er depart
While shouting theirs a brand-new start
That only they can show the way
To bring mankind a better day
So blind they are to never see
Their nothingness can never be

More than the darkness deep within
So, torn and tossed by their own sin
What fools to think they'd ever win
More than the darkness of this life
So filled with pain and self-made strife
That stabs one's soul with molten knife
Yet still they feel that they are right
That they are all by their own might
And filled with self, reject the thought
Their life is nothing, unless bought

For justice does demand a price

And nothing else could e'er suffice

Except for Christ's dear sacrifice

And yet they run their hell-bent way

Believing all their tongues do say

It is the truth, their words do slay

This world continues spiraling down

Within their words, they too shall drown

Amid the pain, the bitter strife

That without God makes up this life

Unless they humbly bow their head

Believing all that You have said

Allowing You to reign instead

Unless by faith they do accept

Their feeble hearts are so inept

Until for sin they too have wept

They cannot ever win life's race

Or gaze upon Your Glorious face

Eternally, to know Your Grace

Whose love by faith our sins erase

Yahweh, Lord the Great I AM

The One True God of Abraham

Jesus Christ, Your Righteous Lamb

How great the pain you must have known!

As Darkness fell—not one light shone

Your wrath for sin poured from your throne

On Your Beloved and sinless son

To Justify each heart You've won

For never could you compromise

Your Righteousness or otherwise

If you forgave and no one paid

Your justice would have been enslaved

And righteousness would only fade

So, looking far beyond Your pain

You focused then upon the gain

Tomorrow's harvest full of grain

Each one You knew would call Your name

You loved so much, you did proclaim

I'll pay their price for all their sin

While justice, righteousness doth win

I see the sorrows that abound
The depths of pain that do surround
Anger, hate the awful sound
And yet, Dear Lord, I know your near
Safe in your arms, I have no fear
There may be pains sometimes down here
Life may have its ups and downs
The angry mobs with hate filled frowns
My love and joy look past the pain
Because You Are My All, My Gain

Preach the word! Be ready in season and out of
season. Convince, rebuke, exhort, with all
longsuffering and teaching.

2 Timothy 4:2 (NKJV)

If I In Silence Do Dismiss

The World cries forth their banner
Diversify, inclusify all manner
Of behavior and thought
Unless you dare to say
Christ died, your salvation bought
Upon the cross that day

Truth is relative they cry
You cannot know the how or why
Unless of course you do proclaim
The gospel message of our God
The freedom found in Jesus name
Then on this truth they trod

Proclaiming it a heresy
Denying their relativity
To justify their rhetoric
They blast you with their words of hate

Ignoring they're a hypocrite
As your thoughts they do berate

If truth is relative as they say
Why would they toss my truth away?
Their passion screaming very loud
To silence every Christian's voice
They flame the fires within the crowd
Denying me my choice

But then, the worst is this
If I in silence do dismiss
My passion for my Lord within
And silently I walk away
Allowing them to die in sin
Never showing them the way

For Grace demands I speak what's true
To everyone who never knew
The love of God, his Grace toward them
No matter what they say or do
I must point each one to Him
By all I say or do

I must sing His name High Above

Telling all about His love

And lay aside all dread or fear

His truth I must always proclaim

My life reflecting Him as near

That they may know Jesus Name

He is the way, the truth, the life

The only way to end all strife

He gave His life to pay my price

Redeeming me in righteousness

No other name could e'er suffice

Transforming pain to joy and bliss.

He is my Lord, my Love, my King

His Glory I must always sing

And never let their words of hate

Silence me, for if they do

Destruction, death their only fate

Unless they come to know what's true

Restore us, O God of our salvation And cause Your anger toward us to cease. Will You be angry with us forever? Will You prolong Your anger to all generations? Will You not revive us again, That Your people may rejoice in You? Show us Your mercy, Lord, and grant us Your salvation.

Psalm 85: 4-7 (NKJV)

A Revival Prayer When Terror Strikes

When terror strikes and fear remains
Tears and blood their mingled stains
That tell a tale of horror's pains
A Broken world so filled with sin
Rejecting God man's heart within
Held tight by pride-those wretched chains

And from the terror hate and lies
That covers all-a dark disguise
To hide the truth and blind our eyes
Man shakes his fist, shouting at God
Whose Grace beneath man's feet was trod
Ignoring He who could make wise

Oh, Lord I bid you hear the pleas
Of all your saints upon their knees
Let our sweet song your wrath appease

Give us the words to then proclaim

With love and truth your Holy Name

Revival then our nation seize

If only they could see Your Face

So filled with love and hope and Grace

Your son who died to take our place

To pay the price that just demand

Before your throne we now may stand

Redeemed, Beloved in Your Embrace

Oh, teach me Lord what words to say

That through my life, You point the way

For others then to come and pray

To find in You the only thing

That then could bid their hearts to sing

Oh, come dear Lord and don't delay

Awaken Lord this heart of mine

To understand Your will divine

Allow Your light of truth to shine

Within my heart, held steady still

Humbly broken then to spill
Forth your love so rich and fine

Give me Your strength to stand the test
Proclaim Your Name to all the rest
No fear or shame to then attest
That Jesus Christ Your precious son
Has Conquered death, the victory won
No other way can man be blessed

And fall before Your Throne of Grace
Humbled, broken to seek your face
Stony hearts of pride You replace
With gentle hearts that seek to find
Your righteousness to fill their mind
Their sin and guilt you will erase

Across the Divide

Amid the clamor between black and white

We scream very loud and think we are right

The bitter divide that comes from each side

Is built on one word-and that word is pride

Yet, humbly each side should look in the face

Of God who has offered to each man His Grace

For God sees our hearts, filled with sin, guilt and shame

Yet, He sent His own son to die all the same

To save us from sin, to pay there our price

Despite all the times, we really weren't nice

Undeserving we stand before His great throne

Redeemed by His Gift given by Grace Alone

And yet, does that mean that some should be free

To riot and kill. How could that be?

God calls us to stand in respect for the law.

Who risk their own lives for one and for all.

We never can be a land that is free

Without laws to guide us, there's no liberty

Only chaos and anger will grow in its place

Until we destroy the whole human race

Can we reach out our hand, to cross the divide?

Instead of closed fists, standing firm on one side

No matter what color, no matter what race

Can you reach out your hand with kindness and grace?

A Prayer for Hope

I heard the cries of the forlorn

The devastation, loss we mourn

While others filled with so much hate

Spewing words, they do berate

They try to say You do not care

Or that You are unjust, unfair

Yet, Lord you reign with Sovereignty

Your justice, righteous clarity

And yet you temper it with Grace

That men might turn and seek Your Face

Open our eyes that we might see

The price You paid to set men free

Oh, Lord, repentant here I stand

How oft I failed Your dear command

To love You first above all things

To raise my voice in praise that sings

Of all Your love and grace toward me

My heart should shout in jubilee!

I pray, Dear Lord, for this our land

That now we would join hand in hand

To lift in prayer as one single voice

Proclaiming that we have made the choice

To sing Your praise from sea to sea

And thank you for our liberty

And when the floods and storms arise

Let us dear Lord, look to the skies

Where there we see Your dear rainbow

A sign of hope to us below

Your covenant is always true

The skies once more will soon be blue

With Him are wisdom and strength, He has counsel and understanding. If He breaks a thing down, it cannot be rebuilt; If He imprisons a man, there can be no release. If He withholds the waters, they dry up; If He sends them out, they overwhelm the earth. He uncovers deep things out of darkness and brings the shadow of death to light. He makes nations great, and destroys them; He enlarges nations, and guides them.

Job 12: 13-15, 22-23 (NKJV)

America Great Again

In dark of night I heard the cries
The moans of the oppressed
Corruption rampant, woeful lies
While truth was ne'er addressed
Our leaders filled with prideful lust
Seeking power to control
Spewed lies of hate and mistrust
That pierced our very soul

BRIDGE:

With no remorse
They set their course
And cried You are all to blame
Deplorable
Irredeemable
They tried to cause us shame
And right before their final blow
The truth we came to know

CHORUS:

Arising then I heard the sound

That rose from shore to shore

Shouts of hope that did abound

As all believed once more

We are a nation built on truth

A bond that holds us tight

The pride of which we taught our youth

It is our strength and might

Awakened now our hearts to sing

Afresh our song of love

As freedom's bell begins to ring

Our flag waves high above

We, the people of this land

Diverse in many ways

As one unite to take a stand

Our minds and hearts ablaze

We slumbered, which was our mistake

Repentant of our sin

Together, hand in hand we will make

America Great Again

President Donald J Trump

For those who still say they do not understand

Why we chose Donald J Trump to lead this land

So, listen really close as I try to explain

How we gladly did board the Donald Trump train

For me it began a few years ago

When I turned on the news, abandoning shows

Up until then with my head in the sand

Accepting in silence the sorrows at hand

At first as I watched and heard CNN

They laughed and they said, he never can win

They would pick out a word, a thought, or a phrase

And talk of nothing else for days and days

The more that they said, "He doesn't belong."

Bigger and Bigger was growing his throng.

As a person who wanted to know what was true

A search for the truth I then did pursue

By listening close to each entire speech

I rejected their "truth"- the medias breach

For when I did hear all that he said

I understood then what had been in his head

I watched as he listened to each person he met

Wanting to know the fears that beset

His heart did transform, his wisdom did grow

He gave of his heart, his hope to bestow

To all the forgotten, the broken, the lost

The victims of rhetoric who bore the cost

Of a social agenda that cut deep our souls

Forgetting all hope, forsaking our goals

He took all the arrows the others could throw

And still stood up strong, letting us know

He was willing to sacrifice all that he had

Because his desire was to make our hearts glad

American pride is what he did give

A hope that in freedom we all can live

He took the time to reach out his hand

To risk everything to then take a stand

It was his heart that drew us all in

To believe in a hope that we all could win

It was his strength, his love, his spirit he gave

America, the land of the free and the brave

God chose this man to lead us today

And nothing you say can cause my heart sway

For I have seen how Satan has tried

Destroying this man as his enemies lied

If only you would take the time to see

The truth of his words, I think you would agree

Donald J. Trump is a man of his word

His love of the people never deferred

By the onslaught of those who seek to destroy

With syrupy words their hate they deploy

Revealing the depth of deceit in their heart

From which they choose their poison impart

To the vulnerable, weak who do not understand

God is the foundation on which we stand

Heroes and First Defenders

Not Tonight

Into the deepest darkest night
Where evil lurks-hid from his sight
An Officer goes-prepared to fight
With all His strength and all His might
Praying to God, not tonight

He gently pulls His children near
Their smiles can lift his heart with cheer
He kisses boo-boos wipes their tears
And as He leaves for work, He hears
Daddy, don't go, not tonight

She kisses him, to work he goes
And all the time, too well she knows
That he must face such evil foes
Phone clutched tight; her eyes then close
Lord, don't let it ring, not tonight

A mother awakens to whisper a prayer
Protect my son from sin's dark lair
Your warrior of truth-just and fair
Endowed by you with virtues rare
He's yours to call, please not tonight

Forgotten and paid a pauper's wage
Media and public he must assuage
While calmly holding back the rage
When violent criminals do engage
Pleading to God, not tonight

These officers protecting you
They sacrifice more than you knew.
When will you value what they do?
Or even stop to say, "Thank You"?
Shame on you, if not tonight

243

"From the Heart of an Officer's Mom"

To My Son

I trembled once so long ago
Upon your first birthday
This world so filled with evil foe
Could I protect your way?

I prayed a little whispered prayer
That God would keep you safe
Protect you from each of life's snares
Give strength to face life's chafe

I see you now, this man you are
Such honor, truth and grace
Your dreams sometimes so distant far
With strength each day you face

I've watched you grow into this prince
So filled with honor, truth
So brave as ne'er at danger wince
Yet gentle, wise beyond your youth

I see you stand before me now
And know what God has done
His wisdom, strength He did endow
For He needed you my son

To be the one, His warrior here
To go into the street
And facing evil's dreadful tear
With justice on your feet

I tremble now as I let go
Upon this special day
This world so filled with evil foe
I can't protect your way

And yet, I know that God above
Will always be your guide
It is His mercy, grace and love
That holds you at His side

Love, Mom

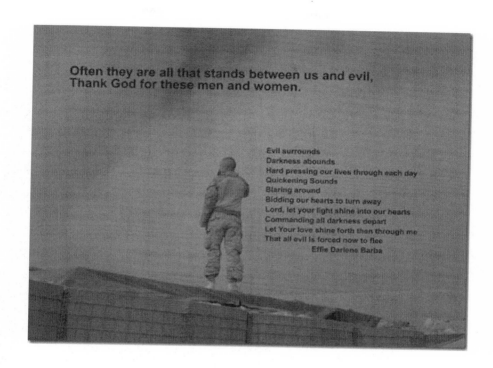

Often they are all that stands between us and evil,
Thank God for these men and women.

Evil surrounds
Darkness abounds
Hard pressing our lives through each day
Quickening Sounds
Blaring around
Bidding our hearts to turn away
Lord, let your light shine into our hearts
Commanding all darkness depart
Let Your love shine forth then through me
That all evil is forced now to flee
            Effie Darlene Barba

247

When you go to war against
your enemies and see Chariotry
and troops who outnumber you,
do not be afraid of them, for
the Lord Your God...is with
you. As you move forward for
battle, the priest will approach
and say to the soldiers, Listen,
today you are moving forward
to do battle with your enemies.
Do not be fainthearted. Do not
fear and tremble or be terrified
because of them for the Lord
your God goes with you to
fight on your behalf against
your enemies Do not be
fainthearted Do not fear and
tremble or be terrified because
of them, for the Lord your God
goes with you to fight on your
behalf against your enemies to
give you victory.
Deuteronomy 20:1-4

A Hero Sat Beside the Grave

A Hero sat beside the grave
His friend was buried there
He wondered if he'd be as brave
When bullets filled the air

A Hero stood beside the bed
A Comrade lying there
"She'll never walk", that's what they said
It all seemed so unfair

A Hero walked-some foreign street
The people turned and stared
Some would run to hide-retreat
While others simply glared

Did others know the choice they had made?
Protect, to serve, to save
Whate'er the cost, their post they stayed
For love, their all they gave

A Hero walked into the room

The doctor standing there

The saddened face, the sense of gloom

An illness, very rare

A Hero stood with stoic grace

Though sadness filled his eyes

The gentle smile upon his face

His broken heart's disguise

These veteran Heroes stood the test

With all that they did do

We must now give to them our best

Our service, our "Thank you"

We cannot see the battle scars

The evil they did face

The pain within their own memoirs

We cannot ere erase

They chose to go for you and me
Because of love you see
They paid the price that we might be
A land where all are free

So, let us sing our anthems loud
Salute the flag with pride
Their sacrifice made us endowed
With hope we're unified

These veteran Heroes stood the test
With all that they did do
We must now give to them our best
Our service, our "Thank you"

This is my commandment, that ye love one another as I have loved you. Greater love hath no man than this, that a man lay down his life for his friends. John 15:12-14 (NKJV)

Because He Loved

He held his wife ever so tight
And kissed each precious child goodnight
Tomorrow early he would leave to fight
For all that's good and all that right

The fight against such evil foe
Is where he knew he would have to go
Defending for us the life we know
For love, his patriotism show

The training never could prepare
A heart and mind so quick to share
For even those who do not care
Who burn the flag and hate declare!

How could it be they hate this land
And the all for which our flag does stand?
Do they not see the dreams they have planned?
Can only be found when evil is banned?

If evil were to have its way

There'd be no place for them to stay

Enjoying freedom's right to say

What's in their hearts or even pray!

And so tomorrow he will leave

Ignoring that his heart does grieve

He would go to battle, no reprieve

For those who do and don't believe

He'd give his life to keep us free

In hope of a world where peace might be

Where good and righteousness we see

To live a life of liberty

So tomorrow he will go to fight

For all that's good and all that's right

He kissed each precious child good night

And held his wife ever so tight

A YEAR LATER

Time passed on and his wife then cried
Tears of such sorrow and of pride
The phone call came that he had died
With many warriors at his side

The men and women fought that day
They held their ground, they would not sway
Their bravery had made the way
For victory to gain a new pathway

He gave his life for you and me
That we might live in liberty
He bravely fought to set us free
Because he loved this land and his family

For God is not unjust so as to forget your work and the love which you have shown toward His name, in having ministered and in still ministering to the saints.

Hebrews 6:10

A Nurse

So Tired and worn she was that day
Slowly now she had made her way
With nothing left that she could say
She fought so hard to save his life
And then explain to his dear wife
That He was gone, gone far away

She held back each and every tear
All the anguish, all of the fear
She gazed into the bathroom mirror
She wore the mask, the gentle smile
That she must wear a little while
For all the patients left to cheer

Tired and worn she left that day
Slowly now she would make her way
With nothing left that she could say
Her feet, shoulders and back did ache
Not near as much as her heart break
She'd hurry home alone to pray

Exhausted now she went to bed
Her whispered prayer was hardly said
Her Bible lay today unread
Her sorrow did her heart consume
And fill the corners of the room
Too tired to think or look ahead

And then it was about midnight
A song arose and did take flight
In darkness there her spirit light
A lullaby from up above
Of God's sweet grace and love
Gave Strength and hope and might

She then awoke at early dawn
Once more to work she would be drawn
Her coffee pushing back her yawn
She donned the uniform once more
As she had all the years before
As off to work she had then gone

258

Today would be a brand-new day
With many words left now to say
A nurse will always find her way
For Angels held her through the night
Instilling strength and God's own might
As Mercy, Love replaced dismay

And as she walked onto her floor
A patient standing by his door
He called her name and called once more
"Thank you, my dear for all you've done
Because of you my battle's won"
Those words then caused her heart to soar

And as she worked on this bright day
She knew the words that she should say
Remembering why she chose this way
A nurse was who she would always be
'Twas more than merely destiny
God chose for her a nurse to stay
He is her strength for each new day

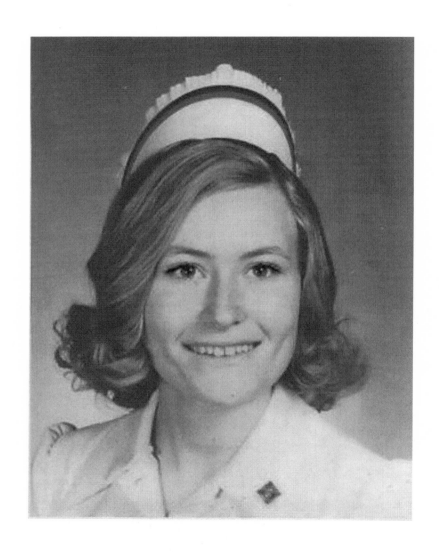

A Nurse I Am

A nurse I am
A nurse I'll be
From my first breath
Through eternity

I feel your pain
Your agony
My heart it beats
With empathy

I'll raise my voice
To fight for you
It's all a part
Of what I do

I will stand strong
To plead your case
No matter what
All else I face

With tender eyes

From years of care

I'll take your hand

Your burden bear

I cannot help

But make this choice

It is my heart

My soul, my voice

At end of day

When weary I

Go home to rest

Sometimes I cry

Then bright and fresh

A new day dawns

I rise with hope

A joyful song

A nurse I am

A nurse I'll be

From my first breath

Through eternity

Bibliography of Bible Versions

(NET) New English Translation NET Bible copyright 1996-2017 by Biblical Studies Press, L.L.C. All rights reserved

(NKJV) New King James Version

Scripture taken from the New King James Version Copyright 1982 by Thomas Nelson. Used by permission All right reserved.

(NIV) New International Version

Copyright 1973, 1978, 1984, 2011 by Biblica

Made in the USA
Columbia, SC
01 August 2020